CATS IN ART

Christopher Wood (1901–30), *Siamese Cats*.

CATS IN ART

Introduced & compiled by
CAROLINE BUGLER

Picture selection by Julia Brown

STUDIO EDITIONS
LONDON

This edition published 1994 by
Studio Editions Ltd
Princess House, 50 Eastcastle Street
London, W1N 7AP, England

Printed and bound in Singapore

ISBN 1 85891 174 5

INTRODUCTION

Frolicking, sleeping, playing or stealing food, cats add their own distinctively appealing note to the most solemn of pictures. Artists always seem to have had a special affinity with these graceful and intelligent creatures, and it is a bond that can be traced as far back as the ancient world. Some of the earliest depictions of cats can be seen in the tombs and papyri of Ancient Egypt, where a cult identified with the cat goddess Bast gave them a sacred status and protected them from injury. Such was the respect accorded to Egyptian cats that when one died it was often embalmed and mummified like a human corpse.

By the first millennium BC domestic cats had travelled from Egypt to Europe via the Mediterranean, where they were probably imported by Phoenician traders. While the Greeks valued them more for their practical uses rather than as pets, the Romans seem to have admired their quality of

William Hogarth (1697–1764). *The Graham Children* (detail). A wide-eyed tabby kitten watches with glee as the bird flutters in its cage.

independence, and there is evidence that they were sometimes used as pictorial symbols for liberty and freedom.

Domestic cats gradually spread to northern Europe, helped no doubt by the legionaries who took them to the corners of the Roman Empire. Although the early Christian church in the West did not much approve of them because of their associations with paganism, they must have been loved by the monks who illuminated medieval manuscripts, since they frequently appear as marginal illustrations in precious works such as the *Lindisfarne Gospels* and *The Book of Kells*. They also figure in medieval bestiaries — religious books written in the form of parables about animals (*see* Plate 1).

The cat's fortunes have been subject to great fluctuations through the ages; during the sixteenth and early seventeenth centuries, at the height of the period of trials for witchcraft, cats suffered because of their associations with evil and Satanism, sometimes being publicly hanged or burned. Yet even at the time of their greatest official persecution, cats never lacked private admirers, particularly among painters. Although they are not actually mentioned in the Bible, cats creep into Old Master paintings of Biblical scenes: they appear in pictures of Adam and Eve in Paradise, the

Fall, the Annunciation, the Marriage at Cana, the Supper at Emmaus, and in pictures of the Four Evangelists. Sometimes they appear in mythological or historical paintings simply to add intimacy to the scene and sometimes they are used in a symbolic way in allegorical pictures. Their characteristics − grace, acuity of sight, agility and independence − have meant that they have been used to suggest a variety of attributes including sight, feminine beauty, earthly love, pride and freedom.

Yet it is in the domestic sphere that cats reign supreme. Some of the finest cat paintings are those showing them in humble interiors of the type favoured by seventeenth-century Dutch artists. Here they appear at their most informal, catching mice, stealing morsels of food, crouching under tables or playing with children. Some Old Masters produced closely observed studies of the animals in action, which were later used in paintings of cats fighting or wreaking havoc with elaborately constructed still lifes (*see* Plate 4).

The eighteenth century saw the rehabilitation of the cat as an object of deep affection rather than as a mouse-catcher or mischief-maker. It was the era when Thomas Gray wrote his famous poem lamenting the death of his favourite cat in a bowl of goldfish, and when Christopher Smart penned

Marguerite Gerard (1761–1837), *The Cat's Lunch* (detail). The cat eagerly laps milk from a saucer in this Neoclassical French painting.

John Morgan (1823–86), *Playing with Kitty* (detail). Cats often appear as children's playmates in Victorian paintings.

his appreciative elegy to his cat Jeoffrey. Artists began to use cats as attractive accessories in portraits of beautiful women and young girls, and sometimes even made them the subject of portraits in their own right (*see* Plate 5).

This popularity continued to grow as the nineteenth century progressed, and cats became treasured hearthside companions in many suburban households. Their increasing respectability was reflected in art, and painters of the stature of Renoir and Manet introduced them to their subject pictures. Just as some artists specialized in horses or dogs, so others chose to concentrate exclusively on cats, usually showing them in domestic situations climbing chairs or pianos, lapping milk or chasing balls of string: Gottfried Mind of Basle, the so-called 'Raphael of the cat world', is one example of this kind of specialist (*see* Plate 6). Sometimes single-minded devotion to cats produced works of extreme sentimentality, particularly among Victorian artists. But in Japan, where cats were just as popular, artists seem on the whole to have avoided mawkish excesses (*see* Plate 9).

Cats have continued to enthral writers and artists into the twentieth century. Amongst French artists they proved especially popular with the painters Suzanne Valadon, Pierre Bonnard and Marc Chagall, while in Britain artists such as Gwen John, Vanessa Bell and Philip Wilson Steer made affectionate tributes to their feline companions. The German artist Franz Marc left over twenty portrait studies of cats (*see* Plate 18). Louis Wain, who was the second President of the British National Cat Club, created a series of caricatures of clothed cats in comic human situations as well as some more serious portraits of cats. However, perhaps more appealing to contemporary tastes are those feline portrayals that stress their animal grace and intelligence, such as Christopher Wood's lovely evocation of two Siamese cats or Duncan Grant's colourful tabby dozing at home (*see* Plate 21).

── THE ──
PLATES

PLATE 1

Bestiary (13th century)
English Manuscript

Three Cats and a Rat

DETAIL

Lat take a cat and fostre hym wel with milk
And tendre flessch and make his couche of silk,
And lat hym seen a mouse go by the wal,
Anon he weyvith milk and flessch and al,
And every deyntee that is in that hous,
Suich appetit he hath to ete a mous.

From *The Manciple's Tale*
GEOFFREY CHAUCER (*c.* 1343–1400)

lapillo imponitur quatuor partibus copulantur. lignoq; in eo-
diuerso locato. dentibz ab aliis hinc inde coherentibz retro
gradeq; trahentibz. ni absq; inuentium admiratione trahūt.

Musio appellatus (Mu-
quod muribz in-
festus sit. hunc
uulgus cattm a captura
uocant. Alii dicunt qd
captat idest uidet. Hā-
cam ātute cernit ut ful-
gore luminis noctis te-
nebras superet. Vnde a
greco uenit catus idē in-
genosus. apotoyka
ɓeszα. Aus.

PLATE 2

Pintoricchio (*fl*. 1481−1513)

Scenes from the Odyssey
DETAIL

For I will consider my Cat Jeoffrey.
For he is the servant of the Living God, duly and daily serving him
For at the first glance of the glory of God in the East he worships in
his way.
For this is done by wreathing his body seven times round with elegant
quickness.
For then he leaps up to catch the musk, which is the blessing of God
upon his prayer.
For he rolls upon prank to work it in.

From *Jubilate Agno*
CHRISTOPHER SMART (1722−71)

PLATE 3

Adriaen van der Werff (1659—1722)

A Cat watching Two Boys

DETAIL

The nature of this beast is to love the place of her breeding; neither will she tarry in any strange place, although carried far. She is never willing to forsake the house for love of any man, and this is contrary to the nature of a dog, who will travel abroad with his master. Although their masters forsake their houses, yet will not cats bear them company, and being carried forth in close baskets or sacks, they will return again or lose themselves.

From *The History of Four Footed Beasts*
EDWARD TOPSELL (*d. c.* 1638)

PLATE 4

Alexandre-François Desportes (1661–1743)

Study of Kittens

Close by the threshold of a door nail'd fast
Three kittens sat: each kitten look'd aghast.
I, passing swift and inattentive by,
At the three kittens cast a careless eye;
Not much concern'd to know what they did there,
Not deeming kittens worth a poet's care.
But presently a loud and furious hiss
Caused me to stop, and to exclaim — what's this?
When, lo! upon the threshold met my view,
With head erect, and eyes of fiery hue,
A viper, long as Count de Grasse's queue.
Forth from his head his forkèd tongue he throws,
Darting it full against a kitten's nose.

From *The Colubriad*
WILLIAM COWPER (1731–1800)

PLATE 5

Francis Sartorius (1734–1804)

Psyche, The Persian Cat

Pet was never mourned as you
Purrer of the spotless hue,
Plumy tail, and wistful gaze
While you humoured our queer ways,
Or outshrilled your morning call
Up the stairs and through the hall –
Foot suspended in its fall –
While expectant, you would stand
Arched to meet the stroking hand;
Till your way you chose to wend
Yonder, to your tragic end.

From *Last Words to a Dumb Friend*
THOMAS HARDY (1840–1928)

Psyche

PLATE 6

Gottfried Mind (1768–1814)

Cat killing Mice in a Landscape

Ten little mice sat down to spin;
Pussy passed by, and just looked in,
'What are you doing, my jolly ten?'
'We're making coats for gentlemen.'
'Shall I come in and cut your threads?'
'No! No! Mistress Pussy – you'd bite off our heads.'

Ten Little Mice
NURSERY RHYME

PLATE 7

Louis-Léopold Boilly (1761−1845)

Gabrielle Arnault

DETAIL

I love little Pussy, her coat is so warm
And if I don't hurt her she'll do me no harm;
So I'll not pull her tail, nor drive her away,
But Pussy and I very gently will play.

I Love Little Pussy
NURSERY RHYME

PLATE 8

Primitive School (1820)

Still Life with Cat and Mouse

Cat! who hast pass'd thy grand climacteric,
  How many mice and rats hast in thy days
  Destroy'd? How many tit bits stolen? Gaze
With those bright languid segments green, and prick
Those velvet ears — but pr'ythee do not stick
  Thy latent talons in me — and upraise
  Thy gentle mew — and tell me all thy frays,
Of fish and mice, and rats and tender chick.

From *To Mrs Reynolds' Cat*
JOHN KEATS (1795–1821)

PLATE 9

Anon. (*c.* 1850)

Sleeping Cat

Dawn follows Dawn and Nights grow old
   and all the while this curious cat
Lies couching on the Chinese mat
   with eyes of satin rimmed with gold.

Upon the mat she lies and leers
   and on the tawny throat of her
Flutters the soft and silky fur
   or ripples to her pointed ears.

Come forth, my lovely seneschal!
   so somnolent so statuesque!
Come forth, you exquisite grotesque!
   half woman and half animal!

From *The Sphinx*
OSCAR WILDE (1854–1900)

PLATE 10

Sophie Anderson (1823–98)

Awake

Dear kitten, do lie still, I say,
I really want you to be quiet,
Instead of scampering away,
And always making such a riot.

From *The Frolicsome Kitten*
JANE TAYLOR (1783–1824) and ANN TAYLOR (1782–1866)

PLATE 11

Auguste L'Orange (1833–75)

Girl asleep with Kittens
DETAIL

A blazing fire, a warm rug, candles lit and curtains drawn, the kettle on for tea… and finally the cat before you, attracting your attention, – it is a scene which everybody likes unless he has a morbid aversion to cats; which is not common.

Poor Pussy! She looks up at us… and symbolically gives a twist of a yawn and a lick to her whiskers. Now she proceeds to clean herself all over, having a just sense of the demands of her elegant person – beginning judiciously with her paws, and fetching amazing tongues at her hind-hips. Anon, she scratches her neck with a foot of rapid delight, leaning her head towards it, and shutting her eyes, half to accommodate the action of the skin and half to enjoy the luxury.

From *The Cat by the Fire*
LEIGH HUNT (1784–1859)

PLATE 12

Johan Caspar Herterich (1843–1905)

Milk for the Kitten

DETAIL

When the tea is brought at five o'clock,
And all the neat curtains are drawn with care,
The little black cat with bright green eyes
Is suddenly purring there.

At first she pretends, having nothing to do,
She has come in merely to blink by the grate,
But though tea may be late or the milk may be sour,
She is never late.

From *Milk for the Cat*
HAROLD MONRO (1879–1932)

PLATE 13

Ralph Hedley (1851–1913)

A Cat in the Window of a Cottage
DETAIL

Years saw me still Acasto's mansion grace,
The gentlest, fondest of the tabby race;
Before him frisking through the garden glade,
Or at his feet in quiet slumber laid;
Praised for my glossy back of zebra streak,
And wreaths of jet encircling round my neck;
Soft paws that ne'er extend the clawing nail,
The snowy whisker and the sinuous tail;
Now feeble age each glazing eyeball dims,
And pain has stiffened these once supple limbs;
Fate of eight lives the forfeit gasp obtains,
And e'en the ninth creeps languid through my veins.

From *An Old Cat's Dying Soliloquy*
ANNA SEWARD (1747–1809)

PLATE 14

Ada Tucker (*fl.* 1881–1928)

A Portrait of a Kitten

DETAIL

That way look, my Infant, lo!
What a pretty baby-show!
See the kitten on the wall,
Sporting with the leaves that fall,
Withered leaves — one — two — and three —
From the lofty elder tree!…
But the kitten, how she starts,
Crouches, stretches, paws and darts!
First at one, and then its fellow,
Just as light, and just as yellow…

From *The Kitten and the Falling Leaves*
WILLIAM WORDSWORTH (1770–1850)

PLATE 15

Louis Wain (1860–1939)

Study of a Tabby Cat

I am the cat of cats. I am
The everlasting cat!
Cunning, and old, and sleek as jam,
The everlasting cat!
I hunt the vermin in the night—
The everlasting cat!
For I see best without the light—
The everlasting cat!

From *The Everlasting Cat*
WILLIAM BRIGHTY RANDS (1823–82)

PLATE 16

Philip Wilson Steer (1860–1942)

Hydrangeas

Stately, kindly, lordly friend,
  Condescend
Here to sit by me, and turn
Glorious eyes that smile and burn,
Golden eyes, love's lustrous meed,
On the golden page I read.

All your wondrous wealth of hair
  Dark and fair,
Silken-shaggy, soft and bright
As the clouds and beams of night,
Pays my reverent hand's caress
Back with friendlier gentleness.

From *To a Cat*
ALGERNON SWINBURNE (1837–1909)

PLATE 17

Beatrix Potter (1866–1943)

Tom Kitten

Tom Kitten was very fat, and he had grown; several buttons burst off.
His mother sewed them on again.

From *The Tale of Tom Kitten*
BEATRIX POTTER (1866–1943)

PLATE 18

Franz Marc (1880–1916)

Two Cats

The cat went here and there
And the moon spun round like a top,
And the nearest kin of the moon,
The creeping cat, looked up.
Black Minnaloushe stared at the moon,
For, wander and wail as he would,
The pure cold light in the sky
Troubled his animal blood.
Minnaloushe runs in the grass
Lifting his delicate feet.
Do you dance, Minnaloushe, do you dance?

From *The Cat and the Moon*
W B YEATS (1865–1939)

PLATE 19

Arthur Heyer (1872–1931)

White Cats watching Goldfish

The hapless Nymph with wonder saw:
A whisker first, and then a claw,
  With many an ardent wish,
She stretch'd in vain to reach the prize.
What female heart can gold despise?
  What Cat's averse to fish?

Presumptuous Maid! with looks intent
Again she stretch'd, again she bent,
  Nor knew the gulf between.
(Malignant Fate sat by, and smil'd.)
The slipp'ry verge her feet beguiled,
  She tumbled headlong in.

From *On the Death of a Favourite Cat Drowned in a Tub of Gold Fishes*
THOMAS GRAY (1716–71)

PLATE 20

Francis Ernest Jackson (1873—1945)

Two Studies of Cats

I muse
Over the hearth with my 'minishing eyes
Until after
The last coal dies.
Every tunnel of the mouse,
Every channel of the cricket,
I have smelt.
I have felt
The secret shifting of the mouldered rafter,
And heard
Every bird in the thicket...

From *The Cat of the House*
FORD MADOX FORD (1873—1939)

PLATE 21

Duncan Grant (1885–1978)

Cat

All that matters is to be at one with the living God
To be a creature in the house of the God of Life.

Like a cat asleep on a chair,
At peace, in peace
And at one with the master of the house, with the mistress,
At home, at home in the house of the living,
Sleeping on the hearth, and yawning before the fire.

From *Pax*
D H LAWRENCE (1885–1930)

PLATE 22

William Gaydon (*fl.* 1936)

A Barn with Cat and Agricultural Machinery

She had a name among the children;
But no one loved though some one owned
Her, locked her out of doors at bedtime,
And had her kittens duly drowned.

In spring, nevertheless, this cat
Ate blackbirds, thrushes, nightingales,
And birds of bright voice, and plume, and flight,
As well as scraps from neighbours' pails.

I loathed and hated her for this;
One speckle on a thrush's breast
Was worth a million such; and yet
She lived long till God gave her rest.

A Cat
EDWARD THOMAS (1878–1917)

PLATE 23

Peter Blake (*b*. 1932)

The Owl and the Pussycat

DETAIL

The Owl and the Pussy-Cat went to sea
In a beautiful pea-green boat;
They took some honey, and plenty of money
Wrapped up in a five-pound note.
The Owl looked up to the moon above,
And sang to a small guitar:
'O lovely Pussy! O Pussy, my love!
What a beautiful Pussy you are, − you are,
What a beautiful Pussy you are!'

From *The Owl and the Pussy-Cat*
EDWARD LEAR (1812−88)

PLATE 24

Ditz (*b.* 1945)

Chicken-Cats

The cat having a mind to make a meal of the cock, seized him one morning by surprise, and asked him what he had to say for himself, why slaughter should not pass upon him? The cock replied, that he was serviceable to mankind, by crowing in the morning, and calling them up to their daily labour. "That is true," says the cat, "and is the very objection that I have against you; for you to make such a shrill impertinent noise, that people cannot sleep for you. Besides, you are an incestuous rascal, and make no scruple of lying with your mother and sisters." — "Well," says the cock, "this I do not deny; but I do it to procure eggs and chickens for my master." — "Ah, villain," says the cat, "hold your wicked tongue; such impieties as these declare that you are no longer fit to live."

The Cat and the Cock
AESOP (6th century BC)

PLATE 25

Robert O'Rorke (*b*. 1945)

The White Cat, Homefield
DETAIL

My Uncle Paul of Pimlico
Has seven cats as white as snow,
Who sit at his enormous feet
And watch him, as a special treat,
Play the piano upside-down,
In his delightful dressing-gown;
The firelight leaps, the parlour glows,
And, while the music ebbs and flows,
They smile (while purring the refrains),
At little thoughts that cross their brains.

My Uncle Paul of Pimlico
MERVYN PEAKE (1911–68)

PICTURE ACKNOWLEDGEMENTS

The author and publishers would like to thank the following artists, collectors, galleries and photographic libraries for permission to reproduce their illustrations: —

INTRODUCTION
Frontispiece: British Museum, London
The National Gallery, London
Musée Fragonard, Grasse (Bridgeman Art Library, London).
Gavin Graham Gallery, London (Bridgeman Art Library)

PLATES
1   The British Library, London (E. T. Archive, London)
2   The National Gallery, London
3   Johnny van Haeften Gallery, London (Bridgeman Art Library)
4   The Fitzwilliam Museum, Cambridge
5   Fenton House, London (National Trust Photographic Library, London)
6   Fine Lines (Fine Art), Warwickshire (Bridgeman Art Library)
7   Musée du Louvre, Paris (Bridgeman Art Library)
8   Gavin Graham Gallery, London (Bridgeman Art Library)
9   Private Collection (Bridgeman Art Library)
10   Christopher Wood Gallery, London (Bridgeman Art Library)
11   Gavin Graham Gallery, London (Bridgeman Art Library)
12   Christie's, London (Bridgeman Art Library)
13   Laing Art Gallery, Newcastle-upon-Tyne (Bridgeman Art Library)
14   Bonham's, London (Bridgeman Art Library)
15   Bonham's, London (Bridgeman Art Library)
16   The Fitzwilliam Museum, Cambridge
17   By permission of Frederick Warne & Co, copyright © Frederick Warne & Co, 1907, 1987
18   Offentliche Kunstsammlung, Basle (Bridgeman Art Library)
19   & Cover (detail) Stern (Art Dealers) Co, London (Bridgeman Art Library)
20   The Royal Academy of Arts, London
21   The Charleston Trust, Sussex © The Artist
22   Cheltenham Art Gallery & Museums, Gloucestershire (Bridgeman Art Library)
23   City of Bristol Museum & Art Gallery (Bridgeman Art Library) © The Artist
24   Private Collection (Bridgeman Art Library) © The Artist
25   Private Collection © The Artist. *My Uncle Paul of Pimlico* by Mervyn Peake, extract from *Rhymes Without Reason* (Methuen). Copyright © The Estate of Mervyn Peake 1944, 1974, 1978